HOMELESS

——I HAVE KNOWN——

Muriel D. Ryan, Ph.D.

BookSide Press
877-741-8091
www.booksidepress.com
orders@booksidepress.com

HOMELESS

I HAVE KNOWN

Dedicated to the love of my life,
my soulmate, and my partner in service to others

Bernard G. Ryan

August 10, 1941 – January 14, 2023

Table of Contents

Preface

Less than a decade ago, I decided to encourage my husband to aid me in using our retirement in service. I must admit that I felt noble in the cause. We would work with the homeless. We would serve families and people without shelter. That sounded simple.

Now, years later, I am humbled that God presented me with this work and said LOVE them. I really wasn't prepared for how much there was to learn. I would learn not only about the homeless and those issues, but about humanity and pain. I would learn not only about courage, homeless children and the issues. Lessons came about loss and depression. I would see dreams gone and painful memories.

In the pages before you are the lives of people who are real. They have lived and walked the streets of cities. They have been homeless in Terre Haute, Indiana, where our organization started. Many came from other cities and other states. As I tell you about them, I might change the name. I might adjust an age slightly. I will protect them not because "it is good professional practice", but because they are worthy of protection. Some, but not all, have already experienced more pain in one life than many of us see.

Yet I will stay close enough to the TRUTH as I can, so you can get to know the homeless. Before we start, I must tell you one of the lessons they have taught me. I use the word homeless when I am speaking to people who have not met a person without shelter before. Homeless is easier. It is faceless. It is anonymous. It allows us to be indifferent. We can generalize, with a broad brush, who these people are. But the ones I have met deserve the dignity of being called persons without shelter. After years, I now begin the first interviews with "How long have you been without shelter?" There is something about saying it that way that makes them lift their faces and look me in the eye. And that is the beginning of each of their stories.

Chapter One

The Lady of Many Firsts

When you start anything, the first opening and first client always sticks in your mind. Nancy and her 13-year-old will hold a special place in the history of the work.and my heart. When we opened Deborah's House as a shelter for women and children after they had been in emergency shelter, they were the first referred to us. They had been at the emergency shelter for longer than most for good reason. Both mother and child had tremendous life-threatening challenges in the nearly 18 months they had been at the Catholic Charities Shelter. Mom had heart problems. They had lost their housing when mom had a fall at work and the employer decided firing was cheaper than workman's compensation. Many times, people lose their homes or apartments because they either don't know their rights or don't have an advocate. They make great efforts to get reemployed, but if you are living paycheck to paycheck that is hard. You would almost have to have a job waiting for you after you get well. And if you must wait to get well, you have normally lost your place to live. So, it was with Nancy and *that* 13-year-old, who both came with glowing recommendations from the emergency shelter.

Now to protect some privacy, this old English teacher will from this point on call the child, "Child". I will also break conventional rules and use plural pronouns such as "their room" to avoid giving away Child's gender. But follow me here because Child was interesting from the day they both arrived.

Amid all the stress of her child's health problems and homelessness, mom had had a heart attack. She had survived it, but it had left her permanently weakened and job hunting was out of the question. Her one desire was to see Child graduate from High School.

Add charm, bright smile, quick wit and being 13 altogether equals and there you have Child.: The world spins around them, but also one who thinks they can stop and start that world at will. Now I must give Child credit for being a good student with a wonderful imagination and the capacity to push rules to the edge without falling over! Mom worked hard on developing sharper parenting skills. So did all the rest of us. Yet that smile and curious nature of Child's personality always landed in a soft place in my heart.

But house rules seemed to trip Child every day. We had set a standard that the children could *not* call the adults by their first name. Child had other ideas. No "Miss Muriel" or "Dr. Ryan" for this child. First name all the way. And then those bright brown eyes would flash, and I knew I had been sucked in again. Child marched to a different beat and a drummer none of the rest of us heard!

Nancy worked on her goals with care and read every book she could get her hands on. Now in her late forties, she deeply regretted previous life choices that had taken a toll on her body. Her weak heart held her back, but she was never one to neglect her chores. Pleasant at all times and patient she was.

She loved the front porch and would sit there reading or watching for hours. One day she remarked that a swing would be nice. I put that idea in the back of my head.

Nancy had wanted better for her children. She had long talks with our Christian head of household. She had lost the path and wanted her children to know God and to follow Him. Nancy began a regular prayer life and peace began to show in her face. It was good to see that. It was good to hear her speak with hope.

One evening in late May, as I was headed to work at a ticket booth at a local festival, she told me that she really liked the artist that was singing at the festival. I was going because our organization raised money by selling carnival ride tickets. She immediately followed her remarks with "I don't have the $10 for the show anyway. You drive careful."

I will never forget that moment. I had a $10 bill in my pocket that she couldn't have known about. I could have taken her as Child was at an overnight sleep over. I could have afforded to do that for Nancy. Within the month I would deeply regret not taking her with me to the festival. She waved as I pulled out of the drive and smiled her big smile.

About two weeks later, I had a late-night call from her housemate. Something was wrong with Nancy. She just wasn't herself. I asked to speak to Nancy. Her voice was a bit different, but I couldn't put my finger on it. How was it different? What was going on? She immediately reassured me that she was fine. Everyone was too worried. Besides, she had a doctor's appointment first thing the next day. I told her I would take her to the doctor's office. She agreed and said she was going to get a good night's sleep.

When I arrived the next morning, she wasn't ready yet. But our first interaction put everything into fast forward motion. Her speech was slurred. She didn't know where the bathroom was in the house. She had lived there for six months. The doctor's office was called to cancel the appointment *after* we called for the ambulance. Child rode with me in my car as we followed it to the nearest emergency room.

Nancy's decline was rapid. Child decided to look for someone to stay overnight with. Word traveled rapidly. Friends started calling in offering to take Child for the night. And Nancy couldn't help. Within four hours after arriving at the hospital, she didn't recognize what a pencil was for. I realized as I watched Child that today their life would change forever. I prayed because I had no wisdom or words that would make the situation any easier.

Hospital protocol for the situation was to contact Adult Protection and Child Welfare. But protocol changes sometimes when the day is Friday, and the hour is 4:30 p.m. Child was going home with me. Nancy was going to ICU. And I was going to become an investigator. We had to find one of Child's two brothers. Gathering up Nancy's address book, contacting the original shelter, and calling the prayer chain at church would be our first steps.

By 10 p.m. that night, all I knew was that the brothers didn't keep track of each other, and I was running out of ideas. Then someone we contacted mentioned that one brother and his pastor dad had recently moved. To this day I praise GOD and the Clinton, Indiana, police department for taking my call and listening to me. "Oh yes," responded dispatch, "now that I think of it, there is a new pastor at the Assembly of God Church and yes, he has an older son living with him." I had found the young man that Child needed, legally speaking.

I am sure I stumbled through the call to the church's pastor as I attempted to explain who I was. It was uncomfortable to share the harder facts, but the words came slowly as he listened quietly. Then he handed the phone to his son. I didn't have the wisdom, but I had a Mighty Counselor. How do you tell a 20-year-old that he is legally first in line to care for a sister and oversee his mother's care after a stroke? I don't know if I did it well, but the support he got from his dad and stepmom was clear from the beginning.

I think back on that day and realize that had these folks not been people of God that Child's life might be very different today. By Monday morning they were in an attorney's office to make all the legal arrangements necessary. Brother was working full time and engaged. I have always wondered how that conversation went with his fiancée. I don't know if that is important though. I do know that Child---Okay---*she* grew up to be a beautiful, bright young woman with a blessed supportive family.

Nancy would linger for about two weeks. As of a welfare patient, her care was less than wonderful. I remember visiting her in a nursing home shortly before she passed. The room was stifling. She was farthest away from the hallway door near the window, but the window didn't open. The air conditioning from the hall didn't reach as far as her bed. She roused that day, just a bit. Her lips were so dry and cracking. I had lip balm and began to put it on her. Her last words to me were "Lips pretty."

The city buried her. But years later on Facebook, I saw a picture of the headstone placed on her grave by the children. She loved them and they honored her. Nancy, you were the first homeless person I really knew. I will never forget you. God rest your precious soul. You now have a permanent heavenly home and I pray it has a wonderful front porch swing.

Pray for peace for both her soul and the souls of her children so they may achieve better lives than Nancy felt she gave them. Those were always her prayers when she arrived. As our first homeless person, you and God taught me to love and serve.

Chapter Two

The Boys

I first met the fabulous Ds at an emergency shelter during a first interview. Mom was a tall, distinguished looking lady. She had six children: an older sister and a younger sister and four boys in the middle. At the first meeting the boys ranged in age from about twelve to eighteen. Mom had them all sit down on the floor in front of me. They looked up at me almost like they were going to worship this short round, Celtic lady. Their dark eyes shined with a soft glow. The only thing missing was the halos that surely were meant for their heads.

About a week later, close to Christmas, I stopped in to check on details for the move from the emergency shelter to our transitional shelter. Mom called the boys down as they were headed to a holiday gathering. The next thing I heard was the deafening hooves of four adolescent males racing down the stairs to get the best seats in the cars waiting for them. Phrases like "Slow down!" "Look out!" "Be careful" etc. rang out in the direction of the boys. I remember tacking myself to the nearest wall while wondering what I had gotten myself into: adolescent boys, great senses of humor and athletics plus more energy than one could find in a strong caffeine drink.

Mom had a thing for same letter for names. She had picked a letter and stick with it. For privacy reasons, I'll pick another letter, but the point will be clear. The boys we will name with Ds: David, Dwight, Donald, and Doug. Bless their hearts, the four Ds were loving and adorable but on any given day they could give anyone high blood pressure. David was always the comic. He, at eighteen, should have been writing for Saturday Night Live! Everything was a joke and every entry into a room required a simulated slam dunk. His most serious side was a determination to grow up and be a good father, which was something missing in his life.

Dwight wore glasses. It suited his whole demeanor. Being of vintage age myself, I always pictured him with a slide rule, lab coat, and a laptop to complete the look. Sometimes you didn't even know he entered the room. He was subtle. A student with sensitivity, he was sometimes a bit lost in the rowdiness of the other three brothers. Although he didn't have much to say, he was wise and sensitive. He could play football and was dedicated to practice. His long legs made him a fast runner. He was the tallest of the four, but with a joker for an older brother, he tended to make the "smallest" footprint within the group.

It might have been my aging or that mischievous grin he always wore, but I could never get Donald's name right. I consistently got it wrong months into their nearly 2-and-a-half-year stay. He seemed to take delight in it. He never gave me a clue. He never helped. He just watched me "suffer" in a good-natured way until one of the others finally shouted it out. He had quite a sense of humor. It was less obvious than his Big Brother's probably because David was built like a lineman and Donald like a running back. *And* David was *King* Funny Guy!

The three oldest were all over age for their grade but still in high school. Doug was middle school age and just about a year older than his classmates. The school decided they needed to "test" Doug. Mom was nervous so I went with her. As an educator I was shocked that the social background study was a one-page sheet done in less than ten minutes just prior to the child study meeting. No mention was ever made nor was any question ever asked about the number of schools he had been in. No one was interested in his being homeless or the impact of homelessness on his academic skills.

After the grown-ups talked, he was brought into the conference. He was asked what kind of **trade** he had considered to *make* a living. I held my breath and hoped he would answer his dream, which was against all odds, but possible with hard work. "I want to be a lawyer," he said. Every jaw dropped with the exception of mom's and mine. The rest of the room looked to be attempting to figure how they could talk him into something else.

The numerous shelters and multiple schools had damaged the course of their education. But a hero was found: Mr. Bernie, also known as The Other Dr. Ryan, retired middle school principal...My Hero M Y *HUSBAND*!

For two trimesters in a row those boys went to school using all his fatherly and professional skill. Like clockwork, he was up at 6 a.m. headed to the women's shelter. First effort was a honk of the van horn. That worked for a while. Next was going inside and calling upstairs. That, too, worked during the early fall, but the weather was getting colder and finally the ultimate "motivation" was used: tossing of four mattresses (*Note: the mattresses lay on the floor*) Doug caught the bus in time and the other three got "principally" driven to school. DR. B used all the skills of enforcement this retired middle school principal still had. While they were with us, the two oldest graduated from high school.

Each of the guys is finding his own path and hugs me every time I see them. I got the last laugh---especially with Doggie. Dobbie? Douglas? Oh, Donald! I once called all the guys together in the front room. Donald came out in a flying leap. Everything in his pocket flew up, but not all of it flew back into his pocket. The condoms fell on the floor. The look on his face as I picked them up was worth ALL the laughs he ever had at me. After an awkward silence, I congratulated him for being smart enough to be safe and waiting for children.

Yes, I will always remember the boys. And they remember me. We remain family by choice. During a recent visit to the women's shelter, they all came by to sign paperwork related to this book; they reminisced, laughed, and talked about their present and their futures. Doug and David and I looked at the house in a quiet moment. Then David said, "*This* was home. Every time I hear that word "home", this is the house I see in my head." One more blessing was added to my life.

By policy, if you leave the program on good terms (kept the rules, did your chores, respected other residents, etc.) you remain part of the family forever, if the resident wishes. Each of the boys---now men—stay in contact with Mr. B and me. They tell us about their children, their jobs, and their dreams. Even with a solid family by birth, they know we are here to support them so neither they nor their children will ever be without shelter again. We didn't want to just aid the homeless for the short term. We wanted to bring homelessness to an end….one client at a time, one family at a time, and we go about it by just loving them. We love them enough to even toss a mattress sometimes.

*Pray that these young men's lives may be
abundant in success and joy. Pray that
each may achieve their greatest life goal:
to be good fathers walking in the steps of
their Heavenly Father.*

Chapter Three

The Separation I Didn't Understand

It began with a call from a local middle school counselor. Most of our referrals to our shelters came from emergency programs, churches, or hospitals. So, this was a bit different. The counselor said she had a mom in her office who said they had run out of money for the cheap hotel they were staying at and were being forced onto the streets. Someone on staff at the school had our business card and knew we did longer term with case management. Though she had never heard of us, since the school was headed into a three-day holiday weekend, she called. God is good. I was only three blocks away.

When I arrived, I met mom. Her eyes were red with tears. The counselor was friendly and began rattling off procedures. I nodded for a while then shortened the lecture on school procedures with a brief history of my vocational and educational path which ended in a PhD and concluded with "you can't tell me much about school policy and privacy laws that I haven't already taught, and fortunately I don't need the information to help this family."

Mom shared with me that they had returned to Indiana with promises of work and shelter which all fell through immediately. Dad, who was so ashamed of their condition, was across the street sitting on a strip mall bench. Daughter was in class still. There were only four days left of the school year. In the back of my head, all I knew was we had NO program or shelter for all three of them to remain together. We had a men's program/shelter and women and children's program/shelter. If we were to serve them, we would have to split them up.

Time left to the end of the school day was sufficient, so we finally got ALL the parties in the counselor's office at the same time. Dad -- who turned out to be Step-Dad-- Mom, and Daughter with the counselor and me. Dad was Walter. Mom was Delores, or "Del" and Daughter was Pepper Ann. "Pep", as mom called her, was cute but clearly stressed. She didn't want to miss the last four days of school because she had made friends. She had been at this school, as I recall, two weeks. She had been at four schools that school year. She last was in this school district four years previously. She looked tired. She looked older than she was. It was sad.

Mom looked like someone who needed a friend, a person she could count on. Of the three, she appeared to be the most stable. Dad could bark an order and she would respond like he was the general. But he didn't come across that way to me. He came across as a coward who was disguised. as a general. He wasn't sold on this idea of being separated. NO, he was not, not one little bit. But our first step was to go see the shelters and see that they were in walking distance of each other. After all, they had been walking 22 blocks twice a day every day, to get Pep to school, then back again to pick her up. I assured them that it wouldn't be nearly that bad in the separate shelters.

As I left them that day with Walt in the men's shelter and Del and Pep in the women's shelter, I pulled off the side of the road. "God, I know it is not your will to tear a family apart, I hate doing this. Please reveal to me what you desire." He soon did.

Within a couple of weeks, the differences were clear. Del and Pep were relaxed and making friends. They laughed and smiled. They worked together with the other residents. On the other hand, Walt was grumpy, complaining he didn't see them often enough. He was caught hoarding hygiene products donated to the shelter. He was just not a happy camper. He tended to befriend the younger residents and not his age peers. With the younger residents he seemed to expect them to comply with his directions with no questions asked.

One night shortly after the fourth of July, Bernie and I got a late-night call from the women's shelter. We went over and took care of a minor issue and realized that Walt had walked in the back of the house with one of the other younger men from the men's shelter. It was after curfew for both houses. When Walt demanded to speak to his wife, I directed him to the backyard. We would meet him back there. He pouted off. He wasn't happy. He wanted to talk to her by himself. Eventually, he and the young male went outside. One of the other moms took charge of Pep.

Walt had it in his mind for the three of them to walk about seventy miles *in the dark* to the next and larger metropolitan city. I called out to the young man who was carrying a small backpack. "Did you know you were going to walk eighty miles in the dark tonight? Do you want to walk eighty miles in the dark tonight?" "*No!*" was the quick response and I said, "Go get in the van in the front of the house." He practically ran!

And then there were three: Walt, Del, and me. I prayed, "What do I do now, God?" "Keep the peace. I'm in charge," came a still small voice. Walt was allowed to stay on the property about six feet away from us until he started shouting demands at Del to go get her bags and Pep. I then ordered him to the alley. He could clearly still be heard. Del kept saying she didn't want to leave. She felt safe here and Walt wasn't on his medicine for his rage. It ended in a stalemate with him in the alley as she was going back inside. And me, I was thinking I was going home.

When I got to the front of the house, Bernie and the young man were sitting in the van. I had just told him to get in the van. I had not said to go back to the shelter. This minor omission in my directions ended up with an extra trip back to the men's shelter after the exhaustion of the backyard conversation. As we headed to the men's shelter to dropped off the young man, he told us how crazy Walt was, but he liked him. Still, he was glad to be going back to the men's shelter.

After dropping the young man off, we decided to make a quick trip past the women's shelter to see if there was still peace. No such luck. In front of the women's shelter were two city police cars and about everyone from inside the women's shelter, including children, there in the middle of the street. It was nearly midnight, and the next day was a school day.

I recognized one officer, and he waved me over. Walt had said we had refused him a last good-bye to his family. I shared more of the details. at the same time the younger officer was interviewing Walt.

The group began to reorganize a bit for this "final" good-bye. Del stood close to Walt who put his arm around her waist. Pep walked over beside her stepdad leaving a space of about a foot. Within a moment, he put his arm around her neck. Nearly losing her balance, she did move a bit closer.

He helped with a nudge to get her closer. Then I saw it. One of those behaviors pointed out in the Minnesota workshops I had been required to take to get my administrator's license. As he tried to nudge her closer and closer, Pep tried to resist by looking down at her foot the farthest from him. She didn't want to be cheek to cheek with him. She didn't even want to be touched by him. She wanted him gone.

The police gave him one last chance and put me in one more bind: Would I let him stay at the men's shelter? Keep the peace. Keep the peace echoed in my ears. "He can stay under one condition. I and his wife believe he is dealing with untreated mental health issues. If he will get an evaluation in the next 48 hours and stick with a treatment plan set for him, he can stay at the men's shelter if he abides by the rules." The senior officer found the plan reasonable and repeated it.

A dead silence was followed by a tirade from Walt about how I personally was trying to break up his family. The senior officer repeated the option once again. Walt avoided any response connected to the option and ranted a bit more. The officer cut off the fruitless effort. Good-byes were said. It looked like a chapter closed. Walt walked the 70 miles that night by himself.

As everyone headed to their vehicles, I passed the younger officer; I made some remarks about our program not being as bad as Walt made us out. The officer smiled. He said, "I know that. I met you when I worked with the campus police, and you were worried about an autistic boy. You guys do good work." God has special ways of reassuring us.

So passed the 4th of July, the school opening, Labor Day, Columbus Day, Halloween, with little more was heard from Walt. He called whining to Del. She described the calls as filled with whining and critical remarks: "You can't live without me." "I'm cold in a tent!" "I miss you." "I hate you."

Del did what she could to protect Pep because she thought Pep loved her "dad" so much. Pep kept her secrets because she felt Del loved Walter.

One day came a reasonable call from Walt which included the announcement that he had enough money for an overnight stay for the family at a local hotel in the city where the women's shelter was. Let's have some family time! There was no reason to say no to an overnight pass. But it just didn't feel right. Walt came to town. They ate dinner at the women's shelter during the day and the three left for a couple of days. After the visit, he headed back to the big city about eighty miles away where he was staying. It seemed like no big deal until conversations started about him coming for Christmas. Then Pep got very quiet. Then self-mutilation started. Then she went to the hospital. The Christmas visit got cancelled.

Mother and daughter were so afraid of hurting each other. Out of both mouths I heard, "But she loves him." And all I could think was "He uses you both." Daughter remained sad and mom remained confused about what to do. In the sadness, Pep became depressed and was hospitalized.

One Saturday, Mom asked me to go to a family therapy session. Every time I had gone, I had tried to interject my "hunches" about Walt, and every time, I got shot down like the slow duck in the formation. Everyone loved poor, sad Walt. But every time he entered the picture this kid hurt herself more. The last time required fourteen stitches. With mom's permission, I got to speak to Pep alone. I don't remember what I said, but it amounted to *now* is the time to tell mom anything you haven't told her. It is important. *Now!*

As we all prepared to leave, Pep asked the therapist to talk to mom privately. Permission was granted. The therapist and I made small talk in the front lobby. Mom came out followed by Pep who hugged her at the lobby door, and they said their good-byes. Mom and I started toward my van. She leaned over a bit. Then she started digging in her purse, I thought for a cigarette. Then I heard a gag, grabbed her hair, pulled it back and everything in her belly came out. There were no words. More like angry grunts with quick bitter phrases. The picture was clear enough to be painful, yet no details were needed. Pep had finally told her mom the whole truth.

They had been moved from state to state. Mom had been forced to work He had claimed he couldn't find work. Pep missed many days of school due to the changes and relocations. All due to a predator now wanted in two states. But that doesn't end the story.

During the worst of the story, Mom found forgiveness from God and was baptized. She decided that if God had forgiven her maybe someone else could and she contacted her first husband. Forgiveness flowed from her first husband *and* daughters *and* grandchildren. Pep found big sisters who loved her and tikes to chase after and a protective man that would be a real dependable adult dude (Dad) that won't let her ever be hurt again.

They would move to the big city and become one very happy big family. Del and Pep were now living with the *real* family where they belonged. One of my favorite pictures of the new family is of this new Dad wearing a t-shirt which says it all: "Faith Never Fails". He must have prayed for years, and God did answer. God wasn't taking apart a family. He was putting the right one together.

EPILOGUE

Walter never really found peace as far as we and his extended family know. He remained mostly untreated and on the streets of a large city. On August 16th, 2015, Del was notified by Walt's family that his body had just been identified. It had been in the County Morgue since June 28, 2014. It confirmed one more time: without treatment, shelter and a constant support system, homeless people die as the result of being homeless.

Pray that homeless children do not fall victim to any abuse.
Pray that those homeless persons find a Godly, trustworthy friend so they can deal with mental illness and do not die as a Joh n or Jane Doe.

Chapter Four

Working hard from day one; does work times two

She looked normal. Other than the fact that she had great blond hair and great blue eyes, life had been rough from day one for her. Choices of men had been "interesting" if I may be graceful. At best it can be said that those relationships had not been successful. Yet, she was the most forthcoming candidate we had at our women's shelter in our first eight years. She was ready for tough choices and change. No hedging. No half-truths. She just laid it out and told it like it was.

She had a sense of the future which meant she made some tough decisions at first. When it became clear that the best paying jobs with the most potential of promotion meant she would have to enter at the night shift level, it was hard, but she did give custody of her boys to their fathers. Then she made sure that every hour of visitation she had was filled with time just for them. She made parent conferences. She prayed and called and stayed in contact. They were going to know that they were *not* forsaken.

Besides working every shift she could get, she became the women's shelter handiest woman. Now I know general construction terms, but she could rattle off the solutions for unbalanced garage doors, flooring, interior doors, and leaky guttering. If it needed to be fixed, she was the fixer. From day one, she worked hard for herself and her children. We never had to set a direction for her. She knew where she was headed.

She didn't stay the entire two years as the best opportunity for her fell into her lap: a fixer-upper was for sale. But about the same time her oldest son's father came down with cancer. The diagnosis was terminal. This father, perhaps, had not been the best role model, but she was not going to steal what good was in the relationship between this son and his father.

She and I didn't talk often, but often enough that I knew she was always wanting the best for her boys: stability, direction, support, and love. When the oldest boy's father passed, we were honored to be called to attend the family wake and dinner. Her son was reading a passage he wrote about his dad. She encouraged him. She let him know how proud of him she was. She reminded him to say "hi" to his dad's family whom he had not seen in a long time.

By now you might have noticed I have not given her a name. I've not even chosen a pretend name. Perhaps that is because a name doesn't seem fitting. Perhaps the right noun or an adjective would do: Courage, Honor, Reliable, Superior Mother, Self-Sacrificing.

Now there was one like her. Our first veteran was female. I remember picking her up. She was *really* homeless. She was living in a muddy trailer with no running water. When I turned off the main road, I remembered making an audible gasp: three trailers on a lightly graveled road which was badly rutted. The entire area was muddy, probably from recent rain. The owner of the property had decided she and her baby added two too many persons in this one trailer. She had to go.

As she loaded the van, everything seemed to be for the baby: stroller, walker, swing, etc. Apart from a few clothes, she had very little for herself. From the beginning, she kept her room clean, watched her baby like a hawk, helped in the house as she could, got a job, and never stopped moving forward. Soon she qualified for public housing and was ready to move on to a permanent situation. She was a worker, not a whiner. She never had pity parties. She was active in her church and participated in many community activities and programs which benefited both her and her son. Note again she is not given a name. Not even a pretend one. That boy of hers breezed happily through toddlerhood as she often posted many pictures of him on Facebook in hopes to encourage others.

Both women are deserving of names that reflect the character they demonstrated from day one. So often people who have never met the homeless mistakenly see them as helpless. Yet talents, hopes and drive can be found in those without shelter. Think of this as a name connected to such people: Determined!

Pray that they continue to seek God for their determination and courage. Pray that homeless programs keep programs structured, while allowing for the highly motivated, talented clients to use their talents.

The dark "aliens" at the door

It was a Thursday afternoon when a call came in from a nearby county which had no shelters. They had a mom and an older teen son who had been abandoned in a city park. Dad had taken off with the family car a night or two before. The older brother had gotten "ticked off" and walked the twenty miles to our city. Now mom and younger brother were looking for shelter. I could take the eighteen-year-old young man in at our men's shelter, but mom would have to seek other option as our women's shelter was full.. The caseworker on and off the phone said that wasn't selling well. I really thought that was the last of the issue.

Then *very* late Friday afternoon, the caseworker called back. The eighteen- year-old was coming. Mom was going to another location. They would drop off the young man. About three hours later I get a call from the house anchor and supervisor: "There are two of them."

"Mom and son?" I asked.

"*No*! Two boys!" he said as he tried to stifle his panic.

With reassurance I told him to put them to bed and I would visit on Saturday morning.

Even with the information I had received from the caseworker, I wasn't prepared for what I saw. Upon arrival Saturday, I met Daniel and John. Immediately, I was struck with how slender, even malnourished they were. It took me awhile to keep straight that Daniel was older yet shorter. John was taller yet younger. Every smile on their faces looked nervous. As I spoke to them, I wasn't sure I was being understood but they kept nodding in agreement. Reports were that they were keeping to themselves, were clean and weren't causing trouble. Also, they seemed to talk to each other in nearly a different "language". By Sunday afternoon, the theory was that they were "aliens" or from Haiti speaking a broken French.

But slowly the facts of their story came out. They had never had a medical exam. They had never gone to school. Their family had declared the four of them a church. Fasting included binging and purging when there was food. John had taught himself basic math and reading. Daniel's goal was to reach the age of twenty-one so he could drink and smoke. When they told stories of childhood abuse, their faces went emotionless and eyes looked as if it happened far off to someone else, much like the facial expressions of Post-Traumatic Stress Disorder patients. And the more they trusted us, the more the stories came.

I would love to tell you that all is well for them. They are physically well. The no-contact orders and involvement of the prosecutor's office made the message to the parents very clear: These young men have voices now and people who would support them in speaking the truth. But the many years of mental, spiritual, and psychological abuse are not easily healed by band aids and surgery.

If you take anything from this book let it be that there are many teens on the street that are there because they can't get the system to believe them, or the parents have kept them out of reach of the system. They may be lucky and "sofa surf", sleeping at a friend's home until they wear out their welcome. They are not all on drugs. These boys, however, had been held in total control and isolation from the world.

When I first talked to the caseworker in this story, she told me that mom had been in her office for a long-time seeking shelter for her and her son who was eighteen. Later she filled in some details: They had been there for four hours. John never said one word. Once when the caseworker stepped away John whispered to mom. When the caseworker returned to her desk, mom asked where the restrooms were. The caseworker pointed. Mom nodded. John went.

Think about that for a moment! John had lost his voice (the sense that one has a right to speak up for oneself) so deeply in the folds of his brain that he didn't even feel that he had the right to ask about a toilet at the age of eighteen! *This is not normal!* It is abuse. He and Daniel are still learning how to deal with their anger, learning that God is Love, and what REAL growing up is all about. It is very hard work for them even working with a team of specialized professionals, staff, and volunteers.

Chapter Six

The Lost Boys

Soon after meeting the "aliens", I met the Adult Protection Division of the prosecutor's office, and they met our program. Normally their case load involves the elderly who are being abused or neglected, but anyone over eighteen being abandoned or needing supervision due to special needs can become a case. We were the only agency with a program which accepts special needs clients on nearly a moment's notice while giving special attention to their needs.

We had one lost boy who was dropped off with his belongings at a larger shelter facility. Within a short time, all his things were stolen or disappeared. We took him to our program and discovered his Social Security was being kept by his mother. She came and got him and two weeks later dropped him off again……at the larger facility.

I remember another young man who I met turned eighteen one week and was unwelcome at home the next. Adult Protection and his father dropped him off at the men's shelter. As his father drove away panic struck him. Like a deer caught in headlights, he froze. But within three days he told a judge he felt loved at our program and Mom and Pop (project directors) were good to him and kept him warm and fed.

Then there was the call from a couple who had met a young man who apparently had Asperger's, a higher functioning form within the autism spectrum. He had become a runaway from a rural community. The couple bought him a hamburger once a week. We placed him in town at the men's shelter, but he needed our special needs program. He and I talked by appointment one day on the nearby college campus. The conversation went well until I mentioned the harm that could happen to someone on the streets. After all, everything he owned had been stolen from him or broken. He picked up his lightweight backpack and pulled out what looked to be a fully authentic service revolver. I noticed the "gun" caught the eye of the security officer in the college library where we were meeting. I asked the boy if I might look at it. He agreed so I stood up and nodded in the direction of the officer. I was so nervous. I don't remember if we approached the officer, or if he came to us. But I do remember keeping the plastic yet authentic looking gun flat in my open palms. I also remember the great relief when the officer took over the conversation which summed up to "something this real looking, boy can get *you* killed."

I remember our first Asperger's Syndrome case that lived in the men's shelter. His mom moved to another state and left him behind. He was very bright but refused to bathe. Personal hygiene was not his favorite part of the day. In fact, he totally refused. And he refused to clean up his food areas. Between the crawly creatures both on him and around him, we had to remove him from the program. Mom, in this case, finally developed a case of guilt. She drove eight hours and took him to a hospital for treatment.

At that time our program was the only emergency intake for mentally impaired and Autism Spectrum patients. We didn't always do it well, but we did it to the best of our ability.

I met one young man at a local hospital as he was recovering from an allergic reaction to bed bugs which he contracted at a different, larger shelter program. Because he had been abandoned, he was considered an emergency which takes six to nine months to get waivers (for the state to pay for services. When the hospital patient first arrived, some of the men in the men's shelter weren't so sure about having him there. He asked the same questions over and over. He sought praise. He needed frequent reminders. He really wanted to please but you had to tell him the same thing over and over. He loved to hug. He asked questions during movies when he didn't understand. But when the time came for him to move to his group home, the guys were full of their own questions, i.e. Can we send him notes? He has our number? Can he call? You're not going to forget us? etc. He had taught them patience, kindness, and love of a simple heart.

If you are a good and faithful parent and have cared for a mentally challenged child for years and completed all the paperwork, i*t takes five to seven years on the waitlist to get the waivers*. Any time a policymaker wants to take me out and explain these policies to me over lunch, I am available. But remember, reader, during the in between time of recognition and policy change, some of them are homeless.

Special needs shelters for these people are few. Again, there are state group homes, but the admission process can become difficult and full of red tape that binds the hands of those parents and professionals seeking to make an appropriate placement. The streets are *not* where they belong. They are vulnerable to those who would take advantage of them, even abuse them.

Pray for those on the street who need specialized care which goes beyond mental health treatment.

Chapter Seven

He Won't Last Six Months

He just kind of arrived. Quietly, like his nature, Dan was just there. The very temporary house anchor knew him from the big shelter in town. He never had much to say. He slept a lot. And he was tall. At 5'2" most everyone is tall to me. But his lanky frame and usually shaved head took advantage of every bit of his six foot plus stature.

At the beginning, he always looked like he was waiting for the sky to fall on him any minute. The day he told me he had a probation officer, he looked like he expected his stuff to be packed and his next steps would be out the front door. He didn't realize we served residents with criminal records. My response was to get the name, rank and phone number of the officer and encourage him to have a good day. The look on his face was a mixture of confusion and relief. He liked not being told to leave but what was this round grandmother-type going to do next after talking to the probation department?

My conversation with Rose, his probation officer, was brief. She had to get his signature on release forms. I indicated I understood.

She had questions about our new men's program and wished me well with an ending message. "He has never lasted anywhere longer than six months."

Reading Rose's materials and more conversations with Dan, I pieced together a life of making poor decisions as a youth, addictions, and the onset of a chronic disease. That was a lot to balance for anyone and it sometimes creates issues within shelters. Housing and feeding are challenging enough. Keeping residents healthy *and* sober gets a little more complicated.

Generally, from the very beginning it was easy to like the resident we called Dan, the man! But he had one very annoying habit: he never missed an opportunity to put himself down. He took the blame for everything. If the sun came up, it had to be his fault. It went from comical to frustrating. One day as I was leaving, he started another "I'm sorry" statement. I turned to make one more joke out of it, then paused. I recalled something I had read in the probation report. His entire introduction to God was as a child with a couple of weeks of Summer Bible School. Suddenly, my mouth opened, and God took over. "I love you, Dan, because God loved you first."

At that point we were about eighteen inches apart. The next thing I knew was an arch of a human being folding over my shoulders. I thought I heard him say something, but my old ears couldn't make it out until he stood up. Tears were running down his cheeks. Apparently, no one had ever told him that. It was quiet for a moment, then he said he wanted to add a goal to his list. Every month residents must make and achieve goals. They aren't huge. But if you make a hundred baby steps, one day you turn around and see you have walked a mile. When I asked him what goal he wanted to add, his response was quick and bright, "I want to hug you good-bye every time I see you."

It may not sound like an earth-shaking goal, but Dan used that goal we mutually agreed upon to march past the feeling that he was to blame for the world's woes and moved on to a more positive attitude. A few thousand hugs and eventually a sliding fee scale mental health specialist started those steps in the right direction.

At this point, one would hope for a happy ending, but that chronic disease held him back. Getting state covered insurance was nearly impossible at that time. He was single. He had no children. Single men with no children apparently did not need health insurance. At least, that was the thinking of policymakers. Disability wasn't coming through for him. Even if you learned from your mistakes, the red tape takes so long to recognize an ailment which had nothing to do with any reckless behavior. Emergency rooms which had seen him before tended to assume he was there for the wrong reason. He had to prove that he was no longer foolish. *And* that he did by taking one day at a time, one blood test after another, speaking up when he was down, keeping active when I knew he was worn. He kept going forward this time, not backward!

Our transitional program normally has a two-year limit, but if the client is actively seeking employment and housing, we will allow a longer stay. Dan took on responsibilities of leadership within the house. He finally got health insurance. He talked more positively about himself. At two years, eleven months, and two weeks, he got into a new housing program for persons with chronic disorders.

I think of Rose's statement often when I think of Dan. He lasted nearly six times longer at Timothy's House, our men's shelter, than he had lasted anywhere else. He learned to sort out what he did wrong from what he couldn't do anything about. Steadily and significantly, He grew in Spirit.

Toward the end of his second spring, a buddy from his youth found him. They had shared some high times. They had stories to share: Dan of his homelessness and local "infractions"; his buddy shared woes from federal institutions now behind him. His buddy thought Dan was dead. Most of the local community knew nothing about where Dan had been in the last two years. His buddy had heard about a new Christian program in the county next door and there at the door stood Dan to greet him.

I suppose I should correct one thing: Buddy wasn't Buddy anymore. He was *Pastor* Buddy, alive and baptized! Dan had been doing some church services in town when his health allowed. Buddy wanted him to come back home to his church so people could see God still does miracles. Dan had risen from the dead.

Dan and I stayed in contact. We laughed over stories about the others that have come and gone from the men's program. He liked keeping track of those who have moved in, were moved on, or moved out. He still remembered what it was like to change the combination on the front door lock when someone decided the rules of the house were there for the breaking. He worked hard to be fair. And yes, he made his goals and then some. He always hugged me when we said good-bye.

Pray for Dan to keep opening the Word. He often says that just opening the pages, a verse will speak to his need that day. Understanding that God loves him so much is still a mystery to him. Pray that daily prayers continue to be a regular part of his bedtime routine.

And pray that doctors will find in wisdom of the Great Physician a means to control his chronic disease which is robbing him of his feet, his strength, and his eyesight.

Chapter Eight

Message to Moms and Dads

When I think of the people represented in these chapters, I see their faces, but I reflect more on their heritage. And a widely varied heritage they do represent. Many were in foster homes. Moms preferred bars and men to their children. Some had parents who represented the opposite end of the narrow spectrum: Parents who never left them alone while never finding anything nice to say.

Many of our female clients were sexually molested prior to the age of sixteen. Some (both men and women) had watched their mothers throw their bodies away and had thought that was the path to follow. Now they faced life with two or three children and no financial or emotional support. Often that repeats in the next generation.

Some saw parents with no compassion. They saw their only value in what they couldn't do, not who they were. The part they couldn't do often led to a disability check for the child spent by the parent. Some of our residents were labeled broken before they entered Kindergarten. To them, being homeless was the final stamp of failure.

They became depressed, confused and without basic skills of living in a positive, supportive family.

As long-term residents, some wanted us to baby them. Others wanted us to give them a place to live where they either took or gave orders, because that was all that made sense to them. Again, this group demonstrated a grave misunderstanding of the word "family".

There used to be a word for moms: Homemakers. Now wait, I'm not dragging you back to pre-WWII, *but* follow my thinking here. With an ever-increasing number of mothers with children becoming homeless, we need to look at how each of us is making *our* home. Does it welcome our children? Does it accept our children and their unique gifts? Does it encourage age-appropriate teamwork? Does it celebrate progress? Does it see family members through tough times? Is the family led by adult role models who have set good examples of values which balance the harshest of standards and the softest of standards? Do the children live in fear, or do they have a voice to respectfully speak up? What kind of home are you making? And while I'm at it…

Message to *dads*…

Woman after woman at our shelter, man after man either don't know their dad, or were tossed out by their dad. Keep your pants on and pulled up! Your sons follow your example. You blame the women, and the women blame the men.

Let's tip the hat to those gents who do take custody

and try raising *your* children. They are called stepdads, grandpas, youth pastors, scout leaders, etc. *These* are DADs, Dependable Adult Dudes.

Now, it is *your* turn to make a home. A lot of times people think being homeless is just not having a roof over your head, but it is so much more than that. A homeless shelter cannot and should not be a way of trying to make up for generations of never having learned what a family is and home is. Blood alone does *not* make a home! These small ones are your children. They are *your* responsibility, parents!

But what if you don't know how to develop that family or home? Try this suggestion: Find a church that when you walk in you feel loved. Watch how people treat each other. Watch how they help each other. If it is a real family, they respect one another. There is no gossiping. They lift one another. And they rejoice when there is something to celebrate. If you don't find all those qualities in the first house of worship you visit, don't give up. Visit another. Christians are called the family of God. By very example, believers should be teaching the making of a home in all ways. Churches, are you teaching family? Make it a priority.

> *Pray that every body of worshipers recognizes their role in teaching, by example, the importance of a good family. Pray we take the messages of love from the Bible and the pulpit back to our homes, so our children know that we walk the talk. Pray for the children who are living in houses where the Word is never heard, or Love is misunderstood. Pray that parents understand that they can directly contribute to their children becoming homeless, when values, wisdom, and love are missing from the home.*

Chapter Nine

The Stinkers!

I am sure there are some readers who by this time have begun to think that I have never met a drug addicted homeless person, a drunk with no shelter, a homeless person with no control over fleshly desires, or any number of other morally challenged people. Maybe you think we have never opened our doors to a thief, a con artist, lazy people, or others that usually create the stereotype of what most persons think of when they hear the word "homeless". Please take comfort in this fact that if you were looking for those kinds of people, I have stuffed them all in this chapter.

They are Stinkers. They leave an odor wherever they go even after a good shower. They undermine peace in a shelter program. They constantly argue. They make it tough for the other residents to trust. They usually think they are smarter than everyone around them. They often bully and intimidate others into submission for any spare money or food. Anything not nailed down, they think is there for the taking. Everything about them stinks! Their values, their attitude, their personality, their language, and their habits all reek and contaminate the atmosphere of the program and the shelter. We served them. We have fed them. We have assisted them with transportation. We have tried to offer them *change* in their lives. Unfortunately, most of them reach that point (in twenty-four hours or less, sometimes) by word or deed when they let it be known that they are not a match to the program.

They have run their lives into a ditch by their choices. Yet, they think they are perfect, and they have nothing to learn. It is time for them to leave.

What do we do with them? We put them out. They are dropped from the program, and they lose their bed. The program has conditions which must be met, or the stinker must leave, even if that requires the assistance of law enforcement. First, they must live by house rules. Every program has rules. We are no different. The rules focus on the importance of living with others and working in cooperation with others. Our shelters are set up like homes. We expect all people to choose to participate in the chores, the planning, and all activities. The shy sometimes take a while to get used to communal living, yet they do. The proud and haughty usually don't last long. We work together on resolving conflict in a manner which respects all parties. They either want to be a part of the "family" in residence or they don't.

Each shelter has a person of great importance: The house anchor. This person is responsible for intake, a great deal of informal counseling, and keeping the property as clean as possible with the aid of *all*. Yes, we go back to the basics. Each resident has chores. We will live together, and we work together.

Stinkers usually are dropped from the program for violation of house rules (found at the end of this chapter), aggressive behavior, bringing illegal items into the shelter, curfew violations and/or theft. Also, we have some that refuse or passively resist doing community service. We expect them to give back to others. It lifts their spirits and reminds them they still have worth.

When stinkers leave, we can make sure they don't come back. In the early years of the programs, we used to give residents keys to the shelter. Wrong move and expensive as most keys never got returned and often meant we needed the locksmith to rekey. But then we discovered the wonderful world of the combination lock. We can show someone the front door and have a new lock combination in place in under 15 seconds, if necessary. We mean business. If you don't want to live by the standards, we don't have to provide you with a bed. We make no apologies for moving people out. You choose your attitude. You choose your use of time. You choose your behavior. You choose your level of participation. If your choices don't line up with our program, there is the door and good-bye.

Perhaps the only place that we are flexible is with those who have addictions. We make every effort to see that no alcohol and street drugs came into the shelter. If found, it is disposed of immediately. We know that alcohol is legal in the state of Indiana for those 21 and older. We know that any addiction is a chronic disease. If someone has had a long period of sobriety, sometimes a trigger (bad news, not being able to visit children, a notice of break-up or divorce, etc.) will cause someone to relapse. *If the resident has been in good standing to that point,* we counsel and bring in support. We add support meetings into their goal requirements. We seek out alternative programs which provide treatment. Unfortunately, in our community, most of those don't come free and most of our clients have little to no financial resources. But our flexibility ends when the person's drunken behavior is of an aggressive nature. We have no place for that. Immediate removal from the program is our step when aggression, either physical or verbal, comes with a relapse.

The other potential problem is idle hands. All our residents at the men's and women/children's shelters must set and achieve goals every month.

At the special needs program, the goals are more prescriptive based on the doctors, mental health specialists, etc. who those residents see. All must abide by house rules which vary little between the programs.

The goals that are set are shaped around our seven areas of growth: Career, Finance, Health, Independent Living, Parenting, Social Relationships, and Spirituality. Each resident must, after the first thirty days, begin their goal book. Each month, they select three areas of growth and determine what they will accomplish in the next thirty days to take those small steps that will eventually add up to a mile. In that mile, they are moving forward and will change. Mid-month, their progress is checked. By the end of the month, it must be achieved, or positive progress must be demonstrated with the evidence of calls they have made, appointments made, jobs they have applied for, new friendships they have developed, etc. You cannot stay in the program if you don't grow.

Many of our residents come to us with immediate needs in health. Lacking a stable environment, proper nutrition, proper rest, and so much more, their initial goals circle around the area of health—both physical and mental. Oh, and here is where my opinion gets thrown in: I do not believe the statistics that would indicate forty, fifty or sixty percents of homeless people have mental health issues. My number would be 100%. Anyone who has been homeless has to deal with the shame and depression that impacts them. This behavior has a severe and negative impact especially on their children. Instability damages the emotional, physical, and educational development of children.

Yes, I have met the stinkers. We present our program as an opportunity to change. When we are interviewing a potential candidate for residence, we try to hit that issue repeatedly. But some people will say anything to get a bed and the opportunity to be a part of a two-year program. We believe that to internalize life changes, two years is a minimum of time. But when the stinker decides to spread a foul odor—at thirty days, six months, a year, or more---we open the door and change the combination. We do that with a clean heart. We provide a letter of warning, a date when the goals must be met, and alternative locations for them to seek shelter. We do the short time, short notice, *now you shall leave* notice when aggressive behavior is displayed.

So, for those of you expecting stinkers among the homeless, you will find them. But with structure and case management setting the pace for a new direction in their lives, you will also find many people who just need a break and support.

Many of the applicants who came to us have either no local family or have burned their bridges with their families. We accept them as people who wish to be part of our family. We strive consistently to be that family of God that will love them with expectations of growth. It is always a blessing, and it happens often. When our residents work hard to change, often reconcile with their blood family.

Sometimes people ask me what we do and how is different from other programs. The answer always comes easily. We love them first. When the stinkers don't like the message, we shake their dust from our front steps and wait for the next applicant who understands why we share the love of God. Our houses were usually full and there was always more work to do. So, we just love them with discipline each day.

"

Pray that staff grow in wisdom, strength, and knowledge. Pray that our staff find sponsors to provide them with a salary. We operate just like a home mission. They must raise their own support. Your contributions are greatly appreciated.

SHELTER RULES

Residents will maintain continuous residence there, respecting a 10:00 curfew daily. * Residents with children will respect a 7:30pm curfew to coincide with bedtimes.

*When work schedules conflict with curfew, adjustment can be made with your house anchor. Still, you MUST be home from work within thirty minutes after your shift is over.

Permission to remain out overnight with family or friends must be obtained from the executive director at least 48 hours prior to any absence.

Each resident will treat all other residents with respect and kindness. Any behavior that creates an unsafe space for yourself and others is unacceptable.

Honesty is expected from all residents. We can't help you if you don't tell us the truth.

Each resident will treat the house and property with care, cleaning up after themselves and completing the tasks on their chore list.

Each resident will take care of and clean their own clothes and living space.

Each resident will assist in meal planning, making meals and cleaning up. This is just one example of the teamwork expected to get household projects completed.

You are not living here alone; you are part of a new "family" by choice.

Each resident, with guidance, will identify personal goals in the areas of parenting (living in a family), career, finance, health, social relationships, independent living, and spirituality. Progress toward these goals will be assisted and monitored by staff. Progress is required to remain in this transitional housing program.

Each resident encourages and supports all other residents in their personal growth, study, and goal achievement.

Negative attitudes, behavior, or other distractions, which undermine the peace in the house, are not acceptable.

The shelter is a sober living environment. The consumption of alcohol or other mind-altering substances cannot be tolerated and can be grounds for immediate dismissal and referral to other programs equipped to manage such problems. We support our residents in their efforts to put substance abuse behind them. Clear minds make better decisions.

Visitors are allowed in common areas ONLY, but must be gone before 8 p.m. Female and male visitors are expected to be always ladies and gentlemen and expected to follow all the house rules as listed above. No visitors (male or female) will be allowed in a bedroom. Be courteous of child(ren's) bedtimes.

The first sixty days of residency are probationary. If you don't fit into the program or we can't meet your needs to grow as a person, you will be removed from the program and must leave immediately. ALWAYS have a backup plan and THINK before you make a bad choice. You can lose more than you realize including your shelter!

Chapter Ten

What I've learned OR What I think God is trying to teach me?

As you can tell from my rather ambiguous title to this chapter, I'm not sure if I am learning or God is teaching. Am I a good student or am I resistant to His directions? I am aware of of things more clearly now, that were not as clear to me before this ministry began. So, before I leave you, allow me to share with you how I am seeing through the glass more clearly.

LESSON #1:

Never miss a chance to do a kindness.

I know that God has forgiven me. I even know that Nancy in her heavenly home has forgiven me. And, though it took a while, I have forgiven myself. When Nancy told me about her favorite band performing, she didn't know I had the price of admission in my pocket. That ten-dollar bill I had stuffed in my pocket just in case I felt a need for a sweet treat. It was never spent that night. Child was at an overnight birthday party. Nancy was free as a bird. All it would have taken was a dose of kindness on my part to give her a special event while I sold tickets at the carnival as a fundraiser for our ministry.

Now it would be like Satan trying to beat me up for this weak moment. But God uses it as a lesson. Kindness is the basic form of love. We should demonstrate it to all we meet. Encourage it in our children. Use it in our language like "Please" and "Thank You". Use it often for the least of these that you might otherwise turn your eyes away from. The homeless are not always a pretty sight, but an encouraging word will brighten their day. But prepare yourself as to what your limit of kindness will be. If you give cash, never expect to see it again. I would encourage you to carry small cards with the telephone numbers of agencies who can help. Never allow anyone you are unacquainted with into your home or vehicle. Allow persons, who work full time with the homeless, to sort the stinkers from the worthy. Even we find that a challenge sometimes. But we start with kindness.

LESSON #2

Patience plus Perseverance Indeed Succeeds!

The boys' mom was in her early 40's and had never learned to drive. Part of that was because she had lived a large part of her life in a big city with a very sophisticated public transportation system. A bigger part of it was she couldn't break through the fear of "what might happen". She didn't have enough faith in herself to learn. Learning to drive was always on her goal list, but I was too patient and did not persevere in my push to get her to accomplish it. Years later I see the result: All four boys entered their twenties without their license to drive. My lack of perseverance with their mother slowed their progress in employment and school. As Paul told young Timothy, Perseverance is key.

Recently, in our women's shelter, I saw a better example of that equation: PA + PE = S! which translated means: Patience plus Perseverance Equals Success!

There was another fear-filled mother who resisted taking the test to get her permit. It was one of her loving housemates who was the persistent one who announced one day, "I'm taking you to the license branch every day until you pass that test."

As it happened, I arrived at the shelter just as they returned from the first try. It didn't go well. Our fear-filled mom looked down until I announced, "I flunked it the first time I took it. Big Deal!" She grinned. We both laughed.

True to her word, her housemate took her the next day. *And she passed.* I got one of the first calls. "I passed!" she shouted. But her housemate's perseverance didn't stop there. Speaking of her persistent housemate, the newly licensed driver next said, "She made me *drive* home!"

Sometimes when we work with people who need "help", we help too much. Never do for them that they can do for themselves. We required our residents to do community service for other agencies. Breaking through the walls of fear, laziness, depression, anger, takes patience. But without perseverance, the necessary quality to break down the walls so they can build new habits requires patience. Yet patience alone may be misunderstood as weakness. The homeless need strong as well as loving mentors.

LESSON #3

No matter how confusing it may seem at first, if it is truly from God, go with it!

God's ways are not our ways. Our ways, as much as we want them to be godly, may not be God's ways. When we look to the Scriptures, we see God using the younger rather than the older, the sinner rather than the church leader, the tax collector over the rich young ruler. When God told me to split a family, even a second marriage family, it made no sense to me. I could not see any wisdom in that effort. It was not until all was revealed that I could see clearly what God both saw and knew from the start. His message to me had been as clear as if it had come in a text message on my phone. Still, it didn't make sense. It was faith that was required to take the steps one day at a time to lead to a clear path of understanding the truth and the message of God's way. Had I fought against His direction, I trembled to think of the damage I would have done to a young girl. I had to trust God's plan. And I am so glad I did.

LESSON #4

When God has given gifts to others so they can give, don't stand in their way.

I feel like I'm about ready to cast stones on other programs, but here goes. When you are housing a person without shelter and this person is about thirty miles (skills, ambition, spiritually, energy, job hunting) ahead of your structured program, you might want to look at your program and make it fit the client rather than make the client fit the program. Both determined women kept curfew, did chores, kept goal books, assisted with activities, and attended Bible studies.

If our round peg expectations were forced on them, when their sprocket was clearly square and functioning at a high-performance level, it would not have been wise, but foolish.

Both ladies understood structure and self-discipline. Those were skills that so many of our clients lacked. Among their housemates, they set good examples. The others didn't complain about them not doing things exactly like they were required to do it, because usually they had done it already and twice as well.

Bottom line, if during the probationary period (ours is thirty days) you see God's gifts flowing, get out of the way and encourage them. God may have sent you the right person at the right time to support you so they might shine before the others.

LESSON #5

Avoid millstone punishment! Report on child abuse and neglect.

Christ told us that if anyone would harm any of these little ones it would be better if they had a millstone placed around their neck and they be thrown into the water. Have you ever seen a millstone? Those things are *huge*. They are very thick and *heavy*. If the knots are secure, you aren't coming up from the bottom of the water. He meant business.

In the state of Indiana, all citizens are mandated reporters. Not just daycare workers, school employees, and pastors. When I saw the brothers, I didn't understand why no one had ever called just based on their weight. They looked like pencils. When the younger one reached 172 pounds at 6'3" after six weeks of healthy eating, we struggled to keep him still eating. He thought he was *fat*. Get involved and save our children. **1-800-800-5556 is the hotline number in Indiana.** Check in your state for the hotline number or call the national hotline number: 1-800-4-A-**CHILD** (1-800-422-4453). Become a foster family, have your church support a foster family, adopt a foster child, have your church support a child in foster care waiting for a forever family. Save our children!

LESSON #6

Just as God sees us each as unique, each homeless person is unique.

If someone had told me years ago that we would need a homeless program for autistic, Asperger's Syndrome, and mentally impaired persons, my first response would have been "*Why?*" I haven't seen them yet. I hadn't heard of them on the street yet. I couldn't imagine parents abandoning them or not having sufficient respite services to deal with the challenges they sometimes present. But they came. One by one, mostly boys came to us with no social skills. Paperwork was incomplete for state support. But the SSI check was floating around somewhere. That was always a mystery. By the way, putting your kid on the street and keeping the check is a crime! We can say that both Adult Protection and the local Social Security office had great faith in our program director. She was the type of bookkeeper who could find receipts from 2007. I, on the other hand, can't find my car keys. But again, that proves we are each unique and so are the homeless.

LESSON #7

You can warehouse the homeless, but if you don't case manage you are not helping them solve their problems. Without goals, they are standing still!

Yes, you can give large groups of people without shelter a bed and three meals a day. But if you can't encourage their growth, they lose. Case management is a fancy two-word phrase used by social workers which means "getting to know them well enough personally to direct them to resources to meet their needs". Once you know their needs, you set goals and direct them to resources.

Now for social workers that would be jobs, housing, health care, mental health services, etc. For a Christian, I see all the above plus supportive new friends with good values, someone to listen who they don't have to pay for, a sense of family that isn't blood related, an advocate that doesn't get paid, and honest friends who hug and tell them the truth even when they don't want to hear it. People who will laugh with you and cry with you. People who will answer the phone at one o'clock in the morning even if it is to tell you you're crazy and things will look better in the morning when we work out a solution. They need people they can trust. This support is often given by a person willing to disciple the homeless.

Homelessness will not come to an end until we recognize that without case management you can't change hearts and you can't change minds. But you can create support systems to keep people in shelters as they grow. It can be done. People just need to know people care. Here is where I call for volunteers to disciple! Across the nation, an outpouring of people willing to donate time to each resident is needed to support clients and shelter programs.

LESSON #8

God is the Father, and we should be talking and

learning about parenting 24/7/365!

The root work of discipline is not *punish*. It is Disciple! Parents, do you disciple your children? Your young children, your middle children, your older children? As they pass through natural development, do you make the changes necessary to respect their growth while keeping them safe?

Are you in every way, every day the example of a *Godly* parent: A shepherd with a hook drawing that child back into safety with the rest of the 99 safely at home? Yes, they are cute at two, but they are big enough to pick up and redirect and tell them "No" firmly---not loudly---but eye to eye. You are in charge. You are the one who sets the rules and the habits for a lifetime. *Do your job!* Don't let others undermine you. Don't be a bully to your child. But love her or him enough to say no, to say you must earn it, you must work hard, you are part of this family, each of us must set a good example. If you don't want your child drug or alcohol filled, there is no place for drugs or alcohol in your life either. You are what they see. They follow you. Your words are strong, but your example is far more powerful. You had or created those children. They are your responsibility. You are no longer a child. *You are a parent. Get a job and provide for your child.*

If it is hard, find a Godly parent or good community resource to coach you. They will forever be thankful for what you do. Please do it early. If you can't handle your children at 5, you need help *now!* Don't let your pride get in the way. Ask for help long before they turn ten because being a teen is right around the corner. Blaming them at that age is easy. As you grow and learn better skills, your child benefits and so does the next generation.

These are just a few of the lessons I have learned. There will be more lessons to be learned. There will be more people to minister to who have no shelter or are hungry. There are paths to follow that God lays before us. Praise be to God as He teaches and guides.

*Pray that effective programs for those
without shelter continue to do God's work
and seek His guidance daily. Pray He
gives wisdom in abundance.*

Appendix

MORE ABOUT FAMILIES BY CHOICE (FBC)

Mission Statement:

Families By Choice meets the basic needs of people at a distance from their family of origin either geographically or emotionally.

The Dream that started it all

In the summer of 2006, I thought I would be retiring, but I'm one who likes to keep busy with new ideas. After much prayer, I had a dream. Like Daniel, Paul, Joseph and others, my dream was clear with names, organizational charts, a place of beginning and long-range plans. I woke up and wrote and wrote. If God had been any clearer, it would have come bound in leather or rolled in a scroll. We were to start housing the homeless with the priority of LOVING them first and holding God's values high. When you get to the values section, you will recognize those values mentioned from Galatians, Philippians, and other Biblical sources.

Each step of the way we stayed true to the original dream: Love the stranger as you take them in. We have been challenged, buffeted as enemies have arisen. Yet God has been faithful, and I have learned to love those enemies more and more.

The "business" function and tax status.

All our shelters allow our clients to stay for up to two years, preparing them to obtain the necessary resources for a move into independent housing.

All our shelters are clean and sober facilities.

(NO DRINKING OR DRUGS ALLOWED)

Families By Choice is recognized by both the State of Indiana and the Federal government as a 501 c 3 non-profit business. Donations are deductible based on the donor's tax status.

Board Adopted Scripture:

Matthew 25:34-36

"Then the King will say to those on his right, Come, you who are blessed by the Father; take your inheritance, the kingdom prepared for you since the creation of the world. For I was hungry, and you gave me something to eat, I was thirsty, and you gave me something to drink, I was a stranger and you invited me in, I needed clothes and you clothed me, I was sick and you looked after me, I was in prison and you came to visit me."

Statement of philosophy and faith of Families By Choice

- When we receive resources from others, we either use them within 90 days or move them on to another agency within our community. We model generosity

balanced with good stewardship in all we do.
- We live and model the faith that has brought us through the hard times of life.
- Recognizing that God's gift to man was free-will, we challenge others to recognize that they must **choose** to live on purpose and not by accident, or letting life just happen.
- Challenges in the life of a person or organization are opportunities to grow stronger and wiser. What we do with those opportunities makes us who we are.
- God has a purpose for us who serve Him and others. To find that purpose we must seek His direction and power.
- We allow the Holy Spirit to develop the details of how individuals will express their faith. Our responsibility is to express love and life- enriching values. We find those values in the Bible.
- We focus on those who desire to grow and change their lives and the lives of children that come into their lives now or in the future.
- Compassion is the core of our motivation. We balance this with accountability.
- Collaboration is how we work and what we model. Competition is not our manner of working or relating to others.
- Compassion and collaboration are both difficult to practice within large numbers. Recognizing that, we will keep our mentor and client ratios near a desirable 1 to 12.
- We will not attempt to duplicate services within the community, but rather offer a patch work

quilt of services from within the community and recognize the gaps in meeting the needs of families and individuals. We respect the Constitutional separation of church and state in our work. Yet, all we do is done to honor and glorify God.

- In all we do, we constantly learn about the poor and the challenges they face.
- We share our learning with all who God brings across our path. Someday we or they might be faced with similar challenges, therefore learning is important.
- Encouragement and edification are more highly desired than condemning and criticism.
- Families of origin are important, yet irrelevant in the services we offer. They may have been ineffective, rebelled against or reached the point of exhaustion. We do not take their place, but rather support people in personal growth and learning how to have healthy relationships.
- Words such as brother, sister, mother, and father, etc. will go beyond the legal terms. We are all children of God and committed to the growth of others who cross our path.
- The work of God may start within the walls of place of worship, yet it is to be lived out beyond those walls. His work with others is our calling.
- Our goal is to honor God and enrich the lives of those within our community. It is not to define perfection in others but seek to be perfect ourselves through our service to them.

Areas of Growth

- Parenting
- Career
- Finance
- Health
- Spirituality
- Social Relations
- Independent Living

Each resident must have a goal for three out of the seven areas each month. Midway through the month's progress is checked by the program director. Residents who do not achieve a goal – also known as a baby step—due to their own neglect or behavior are given a 30-day warning, stating that lack of achievement will result in removal from program and housing. With our goals, we emphasize "Walk a thousand baby steps and one day you turn around and find you have walked a mile."

Values we practice and expect from our residents:

- Faith
- Hope
- Love
- Joy
- Peace
- Patience
- Kindness
- Goodness
- Faithfulness

- Gentleness
- Perseverance
- Truth
- Nobility
- Righteous
- Purity
- Loveliness
- Praiseworthy

Living by these values honors God and produces a positive, forward moving life.

Evangelism

I never thought of myself as being an evangelist. But not long after the first shelter opened, it became clear that if you surround persons with Scripture decals on the walls, lots of donated books written by Christian authors, and regular conversations filled with Bible Stories or verses, it rubs off. I don't know how many times I've said, "You can't build a house (or your life) on a foundation of sand."

Then when we speak of values like self-control, love, etc. the open door to an explanation of the plan of salvation appears in their questions: "Where do you get the strength to hold those values?"

Again, the door is open to explain that Christ has always loved them.

Christ said the fields are white unto harvest. But statistics would indicate that *youth* are the larger population to receive Him. I can assure you I have seen white hair among the homeless. Many have never heard of the Gospel, nor accepted Him. There is a harvest to be gathered in.

Often, I am asked if the program mandates Bible study or church attendance. The answer is no. We allow our residents freewill within the values we hold. We have Bible Studies conducted by volunteers that are not compulsory. Volunteers who lead these studies are concerned about how to get the residents interested. My answer is always the same: "Bring cookies or pizza and be enthusiastic." It works!

Any resident who wishes to eat the snacks are welcome to take a portion but are not required to stay. But they rarely leave. The same is true of Church attendance. We have a list of churches within walking distance of the shelters or ones which offer bus service. House anchors/program directors also point out that attending a church satisfies the Spiritual Goal for the month. Many residents become regular attenders of a church which they find to be welcoming to strangers, non- judgmental of their dress, loving to their children, etc.

We have often prayed for churches to adopt each shelter. Not for money support, but just to come in and love the residents with a pot of vegetable soup, finding out their birthdays and surprising them, playing yard games, etc. Many churches have done just that on a "hit and miss" basis---which is greatly appreciated. Yet we pray that some churches adopt them so that once a month the residents know that beyond staff, others of the Christian faith love them.

Things you can't buy with Food Stamps

When we first opened, I lacked the insight into government programs that I now know clearly. When I realized many residents coming to the shelters with their only resource being Food Stamps. I quickly discovered that we would have to buy toilet paper. You will note it is on the list more than once. Keep this list of needs handy and collect such items for your local shelters

- Hot foods ready to eat,
- Food intended to be heated in the store,
- Lunch counter items or foods to be eaten in the store,
- *All non-food items* (except seeds and plants),
  Including vital household needs:
  - bar soap (For face or bath),
  - shampoo (for adults or babies),
  - hair conditioner,
  - **toilet paper,**
  - deodorant,
  - shaving cream,
  - hand lotion,
  - lip or sunburn protection,
  - *toilet paper*
  - laundry soap,
  - fabric softener,
  - dishwashing liquid,

- paper towels,
- feminine hygiene products,
- ***Did I mention toilet paper???***
- toothpaste
- toothbrushes

In other words, if you use it daily, weekly, or monthly and it is not food, you CAN'T get it with food stamps, even if you do need it to feel clean, look clean, smell clean and live in a clean environment. People with little or no income such as Families by Choice clients, often can't afford these items.

All homeless shelters need a "shower" of these items, every month throughout the year. For many of us, donating the items listed above through our churches or other organizations is easy, but it is an important way to help people put their lives back together. Large sizes for our shelters and smaller sizes of products for our outreach.

PLEASE NOTE

In 2017, due to a sudden decline in my husband's health, we both had to resign from the program, Families By Choice, that we both created and supported for ten years.

In January of 2023, Dr. Bernard G. Ryan passed away with FTD (Frontotemporal lobe dementia). As God orders the events in our lives, shortly after his passing, I was approached regarding rereleasing this book, <u>Homeless I Have Known</u>.

What you have in your hand are the true stories of real people who lacked shelter. At this time, I do not live in the community we served. Yet I am aware that programs and shelters are still doing the work of serving the homeless. It is not my place nor intent to suggest that the following information contained in this book represents presently the practices and positions of that work.

I present it as a guide.

Based solely on what was in place in 2017.